DAYDREAM

Melanie Tran

BookLeaf Publishing

India | USA | UK

Presentation by *BookLeaf Publishing*

Web: www.bookleafpub.com

E-mail: info@bookleafpub.com

ISBN: 9789358739008

First edition 2021

PREFACE

To tell you the truth, I'm scared. Not only is it rare for me to share my writing, but it is also my first time publishing a book! As I write this note to you all, even my family has no clue about how I have decided to publish a book. Surprise! I suppose reaching my twenties sparked something new and eager within me to become more daring and open. With that being said, allow me to welcome you all to a collection of my thoughts.

ACKNOWLEDGEMENT

A sincere thank you to BookLeaf Publishing. Without you, I wouldn't have had the courage to publish and share my writings. Thank you all for the opportunity to share my voice I always kept hidden.

1.

I'm doing well!

Liar.

Just keep on smiling.

2.

Scribble

/ˈskribəl/

1. Unintelligible
2. Messy
3. Chaotic
4. My thoughts & emotions

3.

I-

Nothing.

It's nothing.

4.

I'm just overthinking.

That's what they always say.

I am just overthinking.

I am just overthinking.

5.

Immersing myself within my dream,

I let it swallow me whole.

Enticed by its pure sweetness, I yearn for more.

As I drowned myself in it,

My lungs burned and screamed for air.

Just a bit more, I begged to myself,

While the limbs of my body trembled in this sweet toxicity

6.

While dreaming,

Is it wrong to hope for my nightmares to never meet their end?

When compared, even my nightmares could never overshadow the horrors of reality.

7.

Only through writing may I be able to break this prolong silence of mine.

I want to scream.

8.

If only I could speak as well as I write.

If only I was courageous enough.

If only I wasn't scared of the dark.

If only I wasn't afraid to make mistakes.

If only I accept that I am *enough*.

9.

Like a shadow,

It follows me wherever I go.

Despite its own silence, its influence speaks louder than words.

It follows me,

Not out of hate or despite,

Or even wonder or curiousity,

But fear.

10.

I was born unknowing of the existence of time,

Yet raised to be unable to live without it.

11.

Why do we crave perfection,

In a world that was created to be imperfect?

12.

Like the sun and moon,

I will continue to rise,

To the sky and beyond.

13.

Through day dreaming I escape,

But through escaping do I only hallucinate.

14.

Head always in the clouds,

Sometimes I forget how to return back to reality.

15.

Smile pretty they said,

Smiles half heartedly.

Click. Perfect!

16.

The rising sun may welcome me warmly,

But that doesn't mean the oncoming day will do the same.

16

I was deceived one too many times.

17.

In these day dreams, I let my thoughts flow free,

My desires and wishes revealing themselves,

To me that knows reality won't let them be.

18.

Never knew I would be wanting to run away from the dream I've always wanted most.

I suppose even dreams can become nightmares.

19.

I may not shine as bright as the stars,

Like you want me to,

But, afterall, I can't be something that I am not.

Unapologetic.

20.

Daydreaming I must heed,

Or forever be lost in liminal time.